Vegetarian Slow Cooker Cookbook

Simple | Delicious | Diet Friendly

Kathy Jenkins

Copyright ©

All rights reserved. No part of this book may be reproduced, stored in a retrieval system, or transmitted in any form or by any means, electronic, mechanical, photocopying, recording, scanning, or otherwise, without the prior written permission of the publisher.

Disclaimer

All the material contained in this book is provided for educational and informational purposes only. No responsibility can be taken for any results or outcomes resulting from the use of this material.

While every attempt has been made to provide information that is both accurate and effective, the author does not assume any responsibility for the accuracy or use/misuse of this information.

Vegetarian Fajitas

Ingredients:

3 roma tomatoes, diced

4 ounce can diced green chilies

1 large green bell pepper, seeded and sliced

1 large red bell pepper, seeded and sliced

1 medium onion, sliced

1 1/2 Tablespoon vegetable oil

2 teaspoons cumin

2 teaspoons chili powder

1/2 teaspoon dried oregano

1/4 teaspoon garlic salt

Directions:

-Spray crockpot with a thin coating of non-stick spray.

-Add all of the above ingredients to the crockpot and mix with a large spoon until all vegetables are coated with oil and spices.

-Cook for 4-6 hours or LOW or 2 hours on HIGH.

-Serve with warmed tortillas, black beans, avocado, and sour cream.

Slow Cooker Vegetarian Burritos

Ingredients:

4 cans black beans (14-16oz)

2 cans corn (14-16 oz)

2 white onions, diced

*1 red bell pepper, cleaned and diced

2 cans tomato paste (6 oz)

**1-2 tomatoes, diced

4 tbsp soy sauce (low-sodium is better)

2 tbsp balsamic vinegar

2 heaping tsp cumin

1 heaping tsp thyme

*OPTIONAL

**Can be replaced with one can of spicy, diced tomatoes with chilis

Directions:

Place the onions and peppers (if using) in the bottom of a large crock pot. Pour the soy sauce and balsamic vinegar over them. Set the crock pot on high heat.

Drain the black beans and corn separately. Fill the pot with the black beans, then make a small indentation for the corn in the center. (If the corn's too close to the edges, the corn will burn at this point.)

After 2 hours, begin stirring the mixture every 15-30 minutes. (Before this point, do not stir so that the onions and peppers stay on the bottom getting extra cooked.)

After a total cooking time of 3 1/2 hours, stir in the tomatoes, tomato paste and spices. Continue stirring occasionally.

After a total cooking time of 4 to 4 1/2 hours, the burrito mix will be done. (You'll know it's done when the "dusty" flavor from the cumin and thyme is gone.)

To serve, put two heaping spoonfuls of burrito mix on a warm tortilla. Add salsa and sprinkle with cheese, if you like.

Slow Cooker Mushroom Stroganoff

Ingredients:

500g mushrooms, sliced

1 onion, diced

1tbsp butter

1 stock cube, made up in 600ml hot water

2tbsp tomato ketchup

3tsp paprika

3 cloves garlic, thinly sliced

4tbsp sour cream (heaped)

Handful fresh parsley, chopped

Directions:

In a large pan, melt the butter and gently cook the onion and mushroom for 5-10 minutes, until they are slightly softened and beginning to shrink in size, but are still not yet fully cooked. Transfer these to the slow cooker, and add the stock, kethcup, paprika and sliced garlic. Cook on high for 4 hours.

When cooked, stir in the sour cream and chopped parsley.

If you would like it to be thicker, just transfer it to a saucepan and simmer for 10 minutes to reduce it slightly.

Serve with pasta or rice.

Slow Cooker Bean and Spinach Enchilada

Ingredients:

1 15.5-ounce can black beans, rinsed

1 10-ounce package frozen chopped spinach, thawed and squeezed of excess liquid

1 cup frozen corn

1/2 teaspoon ground cumin

8 ounces sharp Cheddar, grated (2 cups)

kosher salt and black pepper

2 16-ounce jars salsa (3 1/2 cups)

8 6-inch corn tortillas, warmed

1 medium head romaine lettuce, chopped (6 cups)

4 radishes, cut into matchsticks

1/2 cup grape tomatoes, halved

1/2 cucumber, halved and sliced

3 tablespoons fresh lime juice

2 tablespoons olive oil sliced scallions, for serving

Directions:

In a medium bowl, mash half the beans. Add the spinach, corn, cumin, 1 cup of the Cheddar, the remaining beans, ½ teaspoon salt, and ¼ teaspoon pepper and mix to combine.

Spread 1 jar of the salsa in the bottom of a 4- to 6-quart slow cooker. Dividing evenly, roll up the bean mixture in the tortillas (about ½ cup each) and place the rolls seam-side down in a single layer in the slow cooker. Top with the remaining salsa and Cheddar.

Cover and cook until heated through, on low for 2½ to 3 hours.

Before serving, toss the lettuce, radishes, tomatoes, and cucumber in a large bowl with the lime juice, oil, and ½ teaspoon each salt and pepper. Serve with the enchiladas and sprinkle with the scallions

Quick Slow Cooker Vegetarian Eggplant Lasagna

Ingredients:

6 oz Organic Whole Wheat Lasagna Noodles (uncooked)

Eggplant, fresh, 2 medium/large, unpeeled sliced 1/2 inch thick

6 cups Organic Chunky Tomato & Herb Sauce

Spinach or other veggie, frozen/chopped, 1 package (10 oz)

3 oz Part-Skim Ricotta Cheese

1 cup Low Fat Cottage Cheese

½ cup Shredded Parmesean Cheese

Italian Blend Fancy Shredded Cheese (6 servings/bag)

Carrots, raw, 1 cup, grated

Mushrooms, fresh, 1 cup, chopped or sliced

large slow cooker (6 1/2 quart)

Directions:

Spray cooker with pam olive oil

Chop/thaw/squeeze excess liquid from spinach; mix and add to ricotta and cottage cheese

Add carrots and mushrooms to sauce

First layer: add thin layer of sauce to bottom of slow cooker

Second layer: add noodles (break them in order to fit one layer)

Third: sauce

Fourth: ricotta/cottege/spinach cheese mixture (lightly sprinkle with shredded Italian cheese/parmesean cheese)

Fifth: sliced eggplant

Sixth: sauce

Seventh: ricotta cheese mixture (followede by shredded cheese mixture)

Eighth: noodles

Sauce, cheese, eggplant, remaining sauce and cheese

Cook for 3-3 1/2 hours on low (depending on your slow cooker)

Let sit at least 30 minutes

Serving Size: 8 servings

Slow Cooker Vegetarian Spaghetti Sauce

Ingredients:

2 14.5 oz can Diced Tomatoes

14.5oz can Whole Tomatoes

2 tbsp Tomato Paste

Zucchini, 2 medium, sliced in 1/4" pieces

Onion, 1 medium, chopped

Yellow Bell Peppers 1 pepper, chopped

Green Bell Peppers, 1/2 pepper, chopped

Garlic, 3 cloves, minced

Italian Seasoning, 2 tsp

Salt, Pepper & Crushed Red Pepper Flakes to taste

Directions:

Combine all ingredients in slow cooker and allow to cook on LOW for 6-8 hours.

Serve hot over pasta or rice.

Number of Servings: 12

Slow Cooker Vegetarian Paella

Ingredients:

Olive Oil, 2 tbsp

Onion, 1 medium (2-1/2" dia)

Green Bell Peppers, 1 cup, chopped

Green Beans (snap), 2 cups

9 plum tomatoes, chopped (or 28 oz. can)

2 garlic cloves, diced

Artichokes, frozen, 1 package (9 oz)

Beans, Kidney beans dark red 2 cans

Vegetable Stock, 3 cups

Red pepper flakes, 0.5 tsp.

Saffron threads, 0.25 tsp.

Bay leaves, 2

Salt and freshly ground pepper

Saffron Yellow Long Grain Rice, 1 pkg.

Peas, canned, 1 cup

Directions:

Saute onions in olive oil until soft.

Put onions and all other ingredients except rice into slow cooker on low for 4 hours.

Add rice and cook on low for another hour.

Number of Servings: 8

Slow Cooker Corn and Red Pepper Chowder

Ingredients:

2 tablespoons olive oil

1 medium yellow onion, diced (about 2 cups)

1 medium red bell pepper, seeded and diced

3 medium Yukon Gold potatoes, diced (about 3 cups, or 1 pound)

4 cups frozen sweet corn kernels, divided (or fresh corn kernels - approx. 4 ears of corn)

4 cups vegetable broth

1 teaspoon ground cumin

1/2 teaspoon smoked paprika

1/8 teaspoon cayenne pepper

1 teaspoon kosher salt

1 cup soy or almond milk

Additional salt & freshly ground black pepper to taste

Chopped red bell pepper, corn kernels, and sliced scallions to garnish

Directions:

Heat the olive oil in a medium saute pan over medium heat. Add the onion and cook, stirring occasionally, until transparent and soft, about 5 minutes. Transfer the onion to the slow cooker, along with the red bell pepper, potatoes, 1 cup corn, broth, cumin, smoked paprika, cayenne pepper, and salt.

Cook on low for 8-10 hours or on high for 4-6 hours, until the potatoes are tender.

Turn the slow cooker off and remove the lid. Allow the soup to cool slightly. Using an immersion blender or working in batches with a regular blender, puree the soup. Return it to the slow cooker and turn it back on.

Stir in the remaining 3 cups corn and soy milk. Cover the slow cooker and cook on low for another 20-30 minutes, until heated through. Season with salt and pepper to taste.

Serve topped with additional corn, diced bell pepper, and/or sliced scallions.

Slow Cooker Vegetarian Chili

Ingredients:

2 teaspoons canola oil

1 large onion, diced

2 stalks celery, diced

2 carrots, diced

2 cloves garlic, chopped

1 bell pepper, diced

2 tablespoons dark chili powder

2 teaspoons ground cumin

1/4 teaspoon red pepper flakes

1 (29-ounce) can crushed tomatoes

3 (15.5 oz) cans red kidney or black beans, rinsed and drained

12 ounces butternut squash, peeled and diced (about 3 cups)

1 cup vegetable stock

Directions:

NOTE: Sauteing the vegetables before adding them to the slow cooker creates a layer of flavor. Do not skip this step.

Heat the oil in a saute pan, then add the onions, carrots and celery. Saute for four minutes, until the vegetables start to soften. Add the garlic and bell pepper, stir and saute another 2 minutes.

Add the spices and cook for one minute, stirring constantly. Remove the pan from heat.

Add the vegetables and the remaining ingredients to the slow cooker and stir to combine. Cover and cook on low for six hours.

Number of Servings: 8

Taco Soup

Ingredients:

3 (15 ounce) cans Mexican-style diced tomatoes

1 1/2 cups frozen corn

1 (15 ounce) can ranch-style pinto beans

1 (4 ounce) can of chopped green chilies

1 large onion, chopped fine

1 tablespoon fresh cilantro

2 tablespoons powdered broth

1/2 teaspoon chili powder

1/4 teaspoon cumin

1/4 teaspoon thyme

Directions:

Combine all ingredients in slow cooker.

Simmer for three or more hours.

Serve with grated cheese, tortilla chips, extra fresh cilantro and diced onions, shredded cabbage or diced radishes (not included in calorie count)

Number of Servings: 4

Slow Cooker Vegetarian Olive Garden Pasta e Fagioli Soup

Ingredients:

2 packages Quorn Grounds

1 sweet yellow onion, chopped

3 carrots chopped

4 stalks celery, chopped

2 28oz cans no salt added diced tomatoes (not drained)

1 16oz can red kidney beans (drained)

1 16oz can white kidney beans (drained)

3.75 cups low sodium vegetable stock

3 tsp dried oregano

2 tsp ground black pepper

5 tsp dried parsley

1/4 cup whole-drain pasta, uncooked

Directions:

Lightly coat interior of crock with cooking spray.

All all ingredients except pasta.

Cook on low for seven hours or high for four hours.

30 minutes (on high) or one hour (on low) before serving, add pasta.

Number of Servings: 12

Split Pea Soup

Ingredients:

2 cups split peas, rinsed

6 cups hot water

1 cup sliced or diced carrots

1 cup sliced celery

1 medium onion, chopped

2 garlic cloves, minced

1/2 tsp dried marjoram

1/2 tsp dried basil

1/4 tsp ground cumin

1 tsp salt

1/4 tsp black pepper

Pinch of cayenne

Directions:

-Rinse the split peas, then place them in the slow cooker with the remaining ingredients.

-Cover and cook on high for 3 to 4 hours, or until the peas are soft and the vegetables are tender.

Number of Servings: 8

Vegetarian Black Bean Soup

Ingredients:

1 tablespoon olive oil

1 large-size red onion, chopped

1 medium-size red or yellow bell pepper, chopped

1 medium-size green bell pepper, chopped

4 garlic cloves, minced

4 teaspoons ground cumin

1 16-ounce package dried black beans

1 tablespoon chopped chipotle chiles from a can (these chiles give quite the kick, so leave them out if you want a milder soup)

7 cups hot water (your hottest tap water is fine)

2 tablespoons fresh lime juice

2 teaspoons coarse kosher salt

1/4 teaspoon ground black pepper

Directions:

Heat the olive oil in a large skillet over med-high heat. Add onions and peppers and cook until they begin to get soft and brown, stirring frequently (about 6-8 minutes). Add cumin and garlic to the skillet. Stir continuously for about a minute. Transfer skillet contents to the slow cooker, adding the beans, chipotles and hot water. Set your slow cooker on high and cover. Cook for 6 hours, but check at 4 hours because the brand and freshness of your dried beans can affect your cooking time.

When finished cooking, put two cups of the soup into a blender or food processor and puree until smooth, stir back into the rest of the soup. Add in the lime, salt and pepper.

Add a little dollop of low-fat sour cream and some fresh cilantro

Number of Servings: 6

Slow Cooker Vegetarian Stew

Ingredients:

1 medium onion chopped

2 large sweet potatoes chopped

1 medium butternut squash peeled and chopped

3 small sweet/tart apples such as Pink Lady, chopped

1 medium head cauliflower separated into small florets

french lentils, rinsed

1 large can Tomato Puree

1 bunch black kale, chopped

***Salt, Pepper, Cumin, Coriander to taste

Directions:

Chop all ingredients into bite size pieces and place in slow cooker with enough water to come halfway up the sides of the pan. Cook for four hours or until done.

Number of Servings: 8

Slow Cooker Vegetarian Stuffed Sweet Peppers

Ingredients:

1 1/3 cup Morning Star Crumbles

1/2 cup wild rice (long grain)

1 small onion chopped

garlic powder, salt, pepper & italian seasoning - all to taste

2 bell peppers

2 diced tomatoes

parsley (for garnish)

Directions:

Saute Morning Star crumbles with onion - garlic, salt, pepper and italian seasoning. Set aside once cooked through.

In a separate sauce pan -cook rice according to package instructions. Set aside.

In a large bowl mix together Morning Star mixture and wild rice. Add additional garlic, salt, pepper and italian seasoning if needed.

Add about 1/2 of diced tomatoes and mix well.

Stuff each Bell pepper with mixture untill flowing just over the tops. Place in slow cooker

Add remaining tomates on top holding back about 1/4 of them.

Cook on low in slow cooker for about 6hrs.

Place on plates and garnish with parsley

Number of Servings: 2

Slow Cooker Vegetarian Mediterranean Soup

Ingredients:

1 packet Boca crumbles

1/3 cup chopped onion

15 oz can reduced-sodium vegetable broth

1 medium zucchini, coarsely chopped

1 medium tomato, coarsely chopped

1 tbsp lemon juice

1/8 tsp ground black pepper

1 clove garlic, minced (or 1/4 tsp minced garlic from a jar)

2 tbsp crumbled feta cheese

Directions:

In a 2-quart slow cooker, combine onion, broth, zucchini, tomato, lemon juice, pepper, and garlic.

Cover and cook on low for 4-5 hours or on high for 2 to 2 1/2 hours.

Add veggie crumbles during last hour of cook time, so they don't get soggy.

Sprinkle each bowl with 1 tbsp feta cheese before serving.

Number of Servings: 2

Vegetarian Slow Cooker Quesadilla

Ingredients:

2 cups any type of dried beans

1 cup canned diced tomatoes, no salt added

2 cups water

dash of black pepper

dash of garlic powder

1/4 block of firm tofu, crumbled

1 tablespoon of chicken fat (leave out if you're a vegetarian)

2 cups low sodium chicken or vegetable stock

1 whole wheat tortilla,

1 ounce low fat cheddar

1 ounce full-fat Monterey Jack cheese

Directions:

Combine first 8 ingredients in a slow cooker and let sit overnight. In the morning, set the slow cooker to high and let it run for for four hours.

Drain off any excess liquid and set aside the mixture.

Set out tortilla on a plate and add 1 cup of the bean mixture. Sprinkle about 3/4 of the cheese on top. Fold or roll the tortilla and turn over so that the end is tucked under. Sprinkle the remaining cheese on top.

Bake for 2 minutes in a microwave.

Number of Servings: 12

Vegetarian Slow Cooker Onion Soup

Ingredients:

2 Tbsp Olive Oil

5 Large Onions8 Cups Vegetable Stock

Pepper to taste

Directions:

Spread the oil in the bottom of slow cooker, add onions, cover and cook on low for 8-10 hours or longer, until onions are very soft and carmelized.

Add the stock, and season with pepper to taste. Cover and cook on high for 30 minutes.

Number of Servings: 8

Vegetarian Red Beans and Rice for the Slow Cooker

Ingredients:

3 cups water

1 cup dried red kidney beans

1 cup chopped onion

1 cup chopped green bell pepper

3/4 cup chopped celery

1 teaspoon dried thyme

1 teaspoon paprika

3/4 teaspoon ground red pepper

1/2 teaspoon black pepper

2 Morning Star Farms sliced Italian sausage

1 bay leaf 5 garlic cloves, minced

1/2 teaspoon salt

1/4 cup chopped green onions

Directions:

Combine first 12 ingredients in an electric slow cooker.

Cover with lid; cook on low heat for 11 hours.

Discard bay leaf; stir in salt.

Serve over 1 cup of rice per serving ; sprinkle servings evenly with green onions.

Number of Servings: 4

Slow Cooker Vegetarian Jambalaya

Ingredients:

Green Bell Pepper, chopped

Black-eyed peas

Red kidney beans

celery, chopped

Soy Sausage, sliced

Onion, chopped

Canola oil

1/2 tsp Old Bay Seasoning

¼ tsp Dried Thyme

Directions:

Using one tablespoon of the oil, sautee the chopped peppers, onions, celery and garlic until soft (about 5 minutes). Add to slow-cooker stoneware. Add tomatoes, beans, water, Old Bay, Thyme and set slow-cooker on low.

Heat the second tablespoon of oil in a sautee pan and brown the sliced vegetarian sausage on both sides. About 20 minutes before the dish is done, add the sausage to the rest of the ingredients.

Number of Servings: 6

Printed in Great Britain
by Amazon